D1017163

SOS

A Teenage Guide
to Getting
Home in Safety

SOS

A Teenage Guide to Getting Home in Safety

John Bytheway

Bookcraft
Salt Lake City, Utah

Visit us at www.deseretbook.com

ISBN 1-57345-804-X

Printed in the United States of America   72082-6692

10   9   8   7   6   5   4   3   2   1

To my dad,
Seaman First Class Jack L. Bytheway
USS Saratoga CV-3, 1944–1946

Let's go home. Let us prepare to go home to our Heavenly Father's place.

—Yoshihiko Kikuchi,
Ensign, May 2000, 79

There's No Place Like Home

Rarely has a teenager offered a prayer without mentioning something about "getting home in safety." You'd think that the roads to our meetinghouses were infested with bandits, snares, and booby traps. Maybe teenagers use these words because they've heard others use them. Maybe they can't think of anything else to say. But there's another possibility: Perhaps, without their fully realizing it, these sensitive teenage spirits are referring to a different home. A place we used to know. A heavenly place where we walked with God, our Heavenly Father. And they want to return home in safety to his presence.

Eliza R. Snow sensed that, indeed, we are *not* at home when she wrote the words to the hymn "O My Father." She wrote, "Yet ofttimes a secret something whispered, 'You're a stranger here,' and I felt that I had wandered from a more exalted sphere" (*Hymns,* no. 292). It's true, we are strangers here, very far from home, living in an often dangerous place we call earth. Getting home in safety should be our main concern and the focus of all our thoughts and actions.

Strangers in Danger

There was a time, in that "more exalted sphere," when our Father gathered us together and explained that we must leave home for a while in order to become more like him. A Savior was chosen without whom it would be impossible to return. Another who chose to oppose the Father's plan was cast out. We were told that our voyage would be risky, and that some would not make it back home. We were well aware of the dangers, yet we chose the risk. In fact, the scriptures record that we were so excited about our Heavenly Father's plan that we shouted for joy (see Job 38:7).

Now we're strangers here on earth, the memory of those premortal events has faded, and we're preparing to begin our journey home. The dangers are real, they're deadly, and they're all around us. Fortunately, we've been forewarned of the hazards and given strict rules and helpful guidelines to keep us safe. At times, we look around us and consider the storms and the currents and wonder if returning home in safety is even possible. How can we do it? Well, keep the faith. Whenever we doubt our abilities, a "secret something" whispers that everything we need has been provided, and if we seek it, we will receive divine help.

No Mission Is Impossible

Impossible things are not new to Latter-day Saint teenagers. They deal with the impossible every day. They know that with the Lord, things the world considers impossible are possible.

LDS teens have been asked to keep themselves morally clean while others around them are losing their purity and innocence.

LDS teens have been asked to say no to drugs, alcohol, and tobacco while others around them eat, drink, and "party."

LDS teens have been asked to read ancient books of timeless wisdom while others around them play modern video games filled with violence and gore.

LDS teens have been asked to clothe their bodies modestly while others around them disrespect their bodies and parade them before the public.

LDS teens have been asked to rise above the world while others around them sink into the world's immorality and sample all the forbidden things it has to offer.

How can we possibly get home in safety with so many forces pushing us in the opposite direction? We can! It is possible. It is possible because of God.

The sea is dangerous and its storms terrible, but these obstacles have never been sufficient reason to remain ashore....
Unlike the mediocre, intrepid spirits seek victory over those things that seem impossible ... it is with an iron will that they embark on the most daring of all endeavors ... to meet the shadowy future without fear and conquer the unknown.

—Ferdinand Magellan,
explorer, c. 1520

Thou Shalt Construct a Ship...

Compare the difficulty of our earthly assignments to the assignment given to a certain young man we've all read about. He had lived in a Mediterranean desert all his life. Uprooted from his home and friends, he had to wade through affliction in the desert, provide food for his family, and survive near-constant opposition from his brothers. One day, after that family had arrived in a place they called Bountiful, the Lord spoke to this desert youth and gave him an overwhelming assignment: "Thou shalt construct a ship" (1 Nephi 17:8). It was only five words, but can you imagine such a task? The Lord didn't say, "Get some rope and tie together a raft," or "See if you can make a small boat," or "Walk down the shoreline and you'll discover a vessel I have provided," but *"Thou* (that's you, Nephi) shalt *construct* (build with your bare hands) a *ship* (not just a boat, a ship!)." This vessel would have to be large enough to carry his whole family, consisting of parents, brothers, sisters, and their spouses, not to mention supplies and food for the long journey. What must young Nephi have thought as he looked out into the vast ocean that disappeared into the horizon? Yet with powerful faith, Nephi responded, "Whither shall I go that I may find ore to molten, that I may make tools . . . ?" (1 Nephi 17:9). Mr. "Go and Do" didn't believe that God would give him an impossible commandment (see 1 Nephi 3:7). So Nephi "went and did." With the Lord's help, he began to build.

Shape Up and Ship Out!

Each of us has a ship which we must prepare for our journey back home. *Our ship is our life,* and we choose where we will go. We want to live so that our ship can take us home in safety. It's a formidable task. We may be mocked for what we are trying to do, as Nephi was. Some may laugh at us and think that we're foolish, just as Laman and Lemuel laughed at Nephi. Others may look out across the dark, worldly waters and predict our doom. But we will not focus on the negative words of the world. We will focus on the faith-giving words of the Lord.

It's interesting to note that Nephi was commanded to build the ship, but the Lord promised that *He* would bring them to the promised land. Read it carefully: "Thou shalt construct a ship, after the manner which I shall show thee, that *I* may carry thy people across these waters" (1 Nephi 17:8; emphasis added). Only the Lord has the power to save our souls. (*SOS* means "save our souls" in this book.) We can't do it alone. So, like our friend Nephi, when given the overwhelming assignment to get through this world, we'll exercise powerful faith, we will *go,* and we will *do,* and we'll rely on the Lord to bring us home.

Welcome Aboard, Sailor

One more thing before we embark on this adventure on the high seas: I'd like to verbally shake your hand and thank you for being my shipmate. I also want to pay you a compliment. *You*, my friend, are an *extraordinary* teenager. Is that a strange statement to make? (Especially since it's coming from someone who's never met you?) Perhaps. But I think I can safely make the assumption that you are extraordinary for three reasons:

1. You're reading a book, an activity that has become less popular among others your age.

2. You're living on this planet at a critical time period, and your arrival at this place and time was not an accident.

3. You're curious about your responsibilities and anxious to prepare yourself for the chal-

lenges that lie ahead. So not only are you reading a book but you're reading a "church" book.

There's no doubt about it. You are extraordinary. So welcome aboard, my friend, I salute you. Together we'll talk about navigating through the dangers of life and getting home in safety.

That's the end of this briefing. Bring up the anchor, open the sails, and let's get under way.

A ship in the harbor is safe, but that is not what ships are built for.

—John Shedd,
The Forbes Book of Business Quotations,
ed. Ted Goodman (Black Dog and
Leventhal Publishers, 1997), 530

Bon Voyage!

The bowlines and anchors have been retrieved, our sails are filling with the wind, and our vessel begins to move slowly out of port. Our journey has begun.

It might be a good idea to know where we're going before we head for the open sea. No ship ever leaves the harbor without a destination. No vessel ever leaves the shipyard without a rudder to enable it to steer. We are not entering these dangerous waters only to be tossed around like driftwood.

There are plenty of currents ahead to contend with—the "current" fads, for example, the "current" fashions, the "current" morality. We do not intend to be tossed about by every wind of doctrine (see Ephesians 4:14). We know *who* we are, we know *why* we're here, and we know *where* we're going. That knowledge gives our voyage purpose and direction. With our destination firmly in mind, we will cut through the waves like a knife through butter.

Rough Seas Ahead

Some teens have asked, "Why all the dangers? Why couldn't life be easier, and why couldn't we all be saved in the end?" They are good questions. We find some answers in the Pearl of Great Price. After our Father in Heaven presented the plan of salvation, Lucifer proposed that he could be the Redeemer and claimed that he could save everyone. He also sought to destroy our agency, or our ability to choose (see Moses 4:3). Because he rebelled against God, sought for power, and wanted to destroy our agency, he was cast out. In addition to opposing the Lord, he also wants to take us captive. Indeed, we experience opposition in *all* things, and life is tough.

Why couldn't all of us be saved? Satan proposed that he could save us all, but his plan would not have worked. Elder Bruce C. Hafen taught, "Without agency, we *cannot* develop the skills that are essential to the growth we must experience to return to God's presence. . . . Satan's plan *could not have worked*" (*The Believing Heart* [Deseret Book, 1990], 49). We must *choose* to follow the Lord, because God will force no one to heaven. Unfortunately, some may choose other destinations and will not be saved. But that possibility exists because the Lord gave us our agency. And where there is choice, there is also accountability.

You, along with each one of us, had the courage to choose the Father's plan, with Jesus as the Savior, knowing that we would have to pass through all the dangers of this life. Having left the safe harbor of our premortal life, we are watched by the Lord, who is waiting to see what destination we will choose with our agency. It's almost like we're being observed on some kind of heavenly radar: "And we will prove them herewith, to see if they will do all things whatsoever the Lord their God shall command them" (Abraham 3:25).

Greatness is not in where we stand, but in what direction we are moving. We must sail sometimes with the wind and sometimes against it—but sail we must, and not drift, nor lie at anchor.

—Oliver Wendell Holmes

The Gospel of Jesus Christ Is Our Map

Fortunately, although we have no "recollection of [our] former friends and birth" (another line from the hymn "O My Father"), we do have a map to give us purpose and direction and guide us back to the Lord.

Elder John A. Widtsoe explained it like this: "Life on earth is as the large and tumultuous ocean. The chances of shipwreck, or of being driven out of the set course, are many. If, however, the ocean is well charted, the mariners can better avoid the sunken reefs and other dangers, and after the storm can more readily return to the course so that the destined port may be entered with a good bill of health. The Gospel is such a chart, on which the journey of life is outlined, showing the dangers of the journey, the havens of rest and the final destination.

If a man accept the chart, and use it in his life's career, he will find the voyage pleasant and his arrival secure" (*A Rational Theology* [The Church of Jesus Christ of Latter-day Saints, 1915], 45–46).

Elder Widtsoe mentioned not only the dangers of the journey but also the "havens of rest" and the "final destination." Sadly, some teenagers view the gospel as nothing but a long list of do's and don'ts. How unfortunate! They've completely missed the boat. Thinking of the gospel only as a list of things you can't do is like thinking of a library full of good books only as a place where you can't talk. It ignores the most wonderful and important parts!

The Gospel Is More Than the Rules

The gospel is much bigger and grander than a few rules. Sure, there are Standards Nights and *For the Strength of Youth* pamphlets and lessons on chastity, and these are all important things to keep us safe. But the gospel is the good news! It is relief from our sins and problems and afflictions. It teaches us about Jesus Christ, who is the source of peace, happiness, and joy, and the way back home! There is so much more than just the rules, and it is wonderful.

Not only will our gospel map help us steer clear of danger (that's what the rules are for), but along the way we will also enjoy cool evenings of still waters and gorgeous sunsets. We'll feel the sea breeze on deck during the day and "talk of all his truths at night" beneath the stars (see *Hymns*, no. 147).

Man is that he might have joy! That's what the gospel is all about, and if our voyage isn't bringing us joy from time to time, we're doing it wrong. Of course, there will be never-ending happiness when we reach our destination (see Mosiah 2:41), but although life is difficult, we can also find joy in the journey itself.

Some Maps Get You Nowhere Fast

The world's travel brochures offer maps and destinations that bring a short-term, counterfeit joy. Lots of people believe the main things to be sought in this life are popularity, wealth, and a high self-image. They dream about big homes and new cars and a house full of the latest electronic toys.

Some worldly maps lead to clever traps. Perhaps you've heard of the Persian Gulf, or the Gulf of Mexico? Satan wants you to take a worldly course that will lead you to the Gulf of Misery, where he wants you to get stuck. Mormon tells us that laying "hold upon the word of God" will "lead the man of Christ in a strait and narrow course *across* that everlasting gulf of misery which is prepared to engulf the wicked" (Helaman 3:29; emphasis added).

It's easy to imagine worldly rewards. We see them on TV and in magazines daily. But *heavenly* destinations contain rewards so wonderful, so amazing, and so incredible, no one can *possibly* imagine them. If you think worldly treasures sound appealing, listen to the Apostle Paul: "Eye hath not seen, nor ear heard, neither have entered into the heart of man, the things which God hath prepared for them that love him" (1 Corinthians 2:9).

This telestial world is a nice place for a probationary state, but we wouldn't want to live here forever (not until it's been renewed and received its paradisiacal glory, that is).

I wish that every Latter-day Saint could say and mean it with all his heart: "I'll go where you want me to go. I'll say what you want me to say. I'll be what you want me to be." (Hymns, 1985, no. 270.) If we could all do that, we would be assured of the maximum of happiness here and exaltation in the celestial kingdom of God hereafter.

—*Teachings of Ezra Taft Benson*
(Bookcraft, 1988), 344

Choose Wisely!

The Lord wants you to have the *maximum* happiness possible. It's found in following the gospel map and yielding our agency to him. The Lord gave us our freedom to choose, but he asked us to choose him, our Father (see Moses 7:33). What we decide to do with our agency is the major choice of life.

Elder Boyd K. Packer taught: "Most of us have been taught the gospel all our lives. We know the difference between good and evil, between right and wrong. Isn't it time then that we decide that we are going to do right? In so doing we are making a choice—not just *a* choice but *the* choice. Once we have decided that, with no fingers crossed, no counterfeiting, no reservations or hesitancy, the rest will fall into place" (*Teach Ye Diligently* [Deseret Book, 1975], 242–43).

Unfortunately, some teenagers (and some adults) seem to think that they're giving something up if they choose to completely follow the Lord and the gospel map. Just the opposite is true. President Ezra Taft Benson explained: "Men and women who turn their lives over to God will discover that He can make a lot more out of their lives than they can. He will deepen their joys, expand their vision, quicken their minds, strengthen their muscles, lift their spirits, multiply their blessings, increase their opportunities, comfort their souls, raise up friends, and pour out peace. Whoever will lose his life in the service of God will find eternal life" (*Teachings of Ezra Taft Benson* [Bookcraft, 1988], 361).

Owner's Manual for Your Vessel

Much of our gospel map is found in the scriptures and in the teachings of the living prophets. We've been told again and again to read our scriptures. At times you may think all the answers in Sunday School and seminary sound the same, "pray and read your scriptures, pray and read your scriptures," but you know something? It's true. I *know* it's true. Scriptures contain success stories of others who have completed the journey and are now home in safety. Just as we continually study a map to make sure we're on course, we continually study the scriptures to keep us on track in life.

Not only do the scriptures provide a map for our lives, but the very act of scripture study makes us stronger and gives us power. Lots of sailors spend too much time working on the outside of their vessels. They paint and shine and buff and polish. They worry about the fact that their boats are not as sleek as the boats on the magazine covers. Remember that the inside of your craft needs to be strengthened and maintained as well. Scripture study helps you stay in "ship shape" from the inside out!

Speaking specifically of the Book of Mormon, President Ezra Taft Benson remarked: "It is not just that the Book of Mormon teaches us truth, though it indeed does that. It is not just that the Book of Mormon bears testimony of Christ, though it indeed does that, too. But there is something more. There is a power in the book which will begin to flow into your lives the moment you begin a serious study of the book. You will find greater power to resist temptation. You will find the power to avoid deception. You will find the power to stay on the strait and narrow path" (*A Witness and a Warning* [Deseret Book, 1988], 21).

Every Storm Makes You a Better Navigator

Some teenagers may ask, "Well, if we have this perfect gospel map and we know why we're here and everything, how come I still have so many problems?" Good question. Some young people think they're supposed to be happy all the time. The fact is, no one is happy *all* the time. Having the map of the gospel doesn't eliminate the storms and currents and winds. But it does show us the best way to get through them.

Again, we are *not* home. This is the testing part of our existence, and our journey is rough. But we learn more from our trials than we do from our successes. Suppose a sea captain crosses the entire ocean with the wind at his back, with fair weather and smooth sailing all the way. How much less would he know than someone who completed the voyage having gone through hurricanes, headwinds, and hail-storms? Make no mistake about it, we are here to stretch and struggle and strive. There is bad weather ahead, but that's okay. We can weather the storm. That's where our growth comes from—growth we must experience to become more like our Father in Heaven.

"I Wonder If He's Using the Same Wind We Are Using?"

Everyone knows it's windy. The wind blows against every vessel, and the rain falls on the just and on the unjust (see Matthew 5:45). All of us experience adversity. The key is knowing how to respond.

When people encounter difficult trials, they can either draw closer to the Lord or turn their backs and move further away. We always have a choice. In fact, our vessels are capable of moving *against* the wind. This involves a process called "tacking," and it has to do with the set of the sail. President Gordon B. Hinckley observed this process at a lake in upstate New York. "As he watched sailors manage their boats on the choppy lake, he marveled at the way they sailed by turning into the wind and then tacking back and forth. 'It is so with the life of a man,' he philosophized. 'By setting his course and knowing the rules of seamanship as they apply to life, he can move forward and upward even in the face of adversity'" (Sheri L. Dew, *Go Forward with Faith* [Deseret Book, 1996], 358).

In the words of Ella Wheeler Wilcox:

One ship drives east and another drives west
With the selfsame winds that blow.
'Tis the set of the sails
And not the gales
Which tell us the way to go.
Like the winds of the sea are the ways of fate,
As we voyage along through life:
'Tis the set of the soul
That decides the goal
And not the calm or the strife.

("The Winds of Fate," *Masterpieces of Religious Verse*, ed. James Dalton Morrison [Harper and Brothers Publishers, 1948], 314)

The sea of life can at times become turbulent. Crashing waves of emotional conflict may break around us. Chart your course, be cautious, and follow the safety measures outlined. . . . In so doing, we will sail safely the seas of life and arrive at home port— even the celestial kingdom of God.

—Thomas S. Monson,
Ensign, May 1998, 48

From Here to Eternity

So what, specifically, is our destination? Well, we're going home. We want to live with God, and to live the kind of life he lives, which is called eternal life. President Spencer W. Kimball taught: "The map of the gospel of Jesus Christ is made available to the travelers, the destination of eternal life is clearly established. At that destination our Father waits hopefully, anxious to greet his returning children" (*The Miracle of Forgiveness* [Bookcraft, 1969], 19).

Again, no ship ever left the port without a destination. We would be wise navigators to plan the whole trip in the captain's cabin before we set sail. Elder Joseph B. Wirthlin taught: "You should look ahead now and decide what you want to do with your lives. Fix clearly in your mind what you want to be one year from

now, five years, ten years, and beyond. . . .
Write your goals and review them regularly.
Keep them before you constantly, record your
progress, and revise them as circumstances dic-
tate. Your ultimate goals should be eternal life—
the kind of life God lives, the greatest of all the
gifts of God" (*Ensign,* November 1989, 73).

Built for Adventure

I repeat the words of John Shedd, "A ship in the harbor is safe, but that is not what ships are built for."

We have made our choice. We have set sail. We're out of the harbor and into the fray. We will meet the world head-on, and in the strength of the Lord, we will succeed. Elder Boyd K. Packer remarked, "It is my conviction that your generation is better and stronger than was ours—better in many ways! I have faith that you young men and young women can meet the world on its own terms and conquer it!" (*Ensign,* May 1989, 54).

We have no intention of being caught in modern society's currents with no map, no compass, and no direction. We are not adrift on an old log. We have a *ship,* we have a *map,* and we have a *destination*—eternal life.

Speaking of storms, there's one ahead. Black clouds, wind, and rain off the port bow! Batten down the hatches, mates—we're going in.

Constancy Amid Change

When we sail into bad weather, everything around us is in constant commotion. The waves toss our vessel to and fro; the winds shift suddenly and howl around our sails. The rain makes it difficult to see ahead. What do we do in cases like that? We can't find our place on the map, we can't see the position of the stars, and we can't even see what's ahead because of the downpour.

Lots of things on our voyage are constantly changing—the currents, the winds, the weather. Fortunately, we also have a few things we can count on that *never* change. These constants help us keep our bearings. They keep us from getting lost. They include our *compass,* the *lighthouse,* and our *anchor.*

Before the invention of the compass, mariners either kept their vessels within sight of land or got their position from the stars. But the stars are only visible in clear weather. Because of these limitations, they never got very far.

We are blessed because a compass works in any kind of weather, and each of us has our very own. The light of Christ is like a compass. It is given to *everyone* and can lead one to do what is right, accept the gospel, and eventually receive a greater gift, the gift of the Holy Ghost.

*Any youth without religious convictions
and lacking a faith in eternal values is as a
sailor without a compass or as a
traveler without a guide.*

—Harold B. Lee,
Decisions for Successful Living
(Deseret Book, 1973), 8

Dad, I Salute You!

In the front of this book, you saw a picture of my father. He joined the Navy on his eighteenth birthday and served aboard an aircraft carrier in World War II. He was not a member of the Church at the time. My father had never attended a Standards Night or read a *For the Strength of Youth* pamphlet. When I asked him why he didn't get in trouble with immorality like many of the other sailors, he replied, "I thought it would disappoint my dad."

I'm proud of my father because, although he didn't know what it was called, he responded to the light of Christ within him. His internal compass would not allow him to be swept into the current of immoral behavior.

After the war, he met a girl who introduced him to the gospel. He investigated the Church, gained a testimony, submitted to baptism, received the gift of the Holy Ghost, and married the young woman (my mom). Shortly after they were married, he was called to serve a mission in New England.

Elder James E. Faust taught: "The gift of the Holy Ghost is available as a sure guide, as the voice of conscience, and as a moral compass. This guiding compass is personal to each of us. It is unerring. It is unfailing. However, we must listen to it in order to steer clear of the shoals that can cause our lives to sink into unhappiness and self-doubt" (*Reach Up for the Light* [Deseret Book, 1990], 118).

Dad, thanks for being true to your compass. Like you, I don't want to disappoint *my* dad, so I'll try to follow my compass as faithfully as you did!

One Wave at a Time

Not only do we enjoy the light of Christ, but you and I have been given the gift of the Holy Ghost, which is the right to the *constant* companionship of the Holy Ghost, based on our faithfulness. What a wonderful gift, and what a powerful compass!

Sometimes we have to navigate through the waves one at a time. A map is a long-range tool, but waves have to be taken as they come. Part of our journey involves making small decisions. You're aware that your final destination is eternal life. But how does that knowledge help you in the hall at high school? How does it help you at a party when the peer pressure is on and you don't know what to do? Eternal life is our long-range goal, but sometimes we need specific direction on daily decisions. That's where the compass of the Holy Ghost comes in.

Several years after Joseph Smith was martyred, he appeared to Brigham Young in a dream or vision and said: "Tell the people to be humble and faithful, and be sure to keep the spirit of the Lord and it will lead them right. Be careful and not turn away the still small voice; it will teach you what to do and where to go" (*Manuscript History of Brigham Young: 1846–47* [Historical Department, The Church of Jesus Christ of Latter-day Saints], n.p.).

It's impossible to suggest a course of action for every peer pressure situation. But you have the right to constant help! Keep an eye on your compass, in big decisions and small ones, and it will lead you right.

Overconfident, Overwhelmed, and Overboard

Well, mates, we've been at sea for several days now, and our voyage has been glorious. We've pressed on through rain and fog, weathered blinding storms, and survived chilling blizzards. Our confidence has grown with each day at sea as we journey home.

But there's something ominous ahead. It's more foreboding than anything we've seen thus far. The clouds are dark and towering. A scan of the horizon reveals whitecaps on the waves. We'd better bring in the sails or these winds will rip them to shreds.

Moving into the storm, we're on high alert. Waves crash against the bow like watery mountains trying to bury us in the deep. They are relentless. Hour after hour they come, one after another. Our strength is exhausted, and we're soaked to the skin. Lightning flashes, thunder echoes, and saltwater crashes across the desk with every swell. How long can we endure this on our own?

The situation becomes critical. Suddenly, we come to the horrifying conclusion that we must give the order, *"Abandon ship, abandon ship!"* How could this happen? What went wrong? We were so confident as we put out to sea! We thought we had everything we needed! We thought we were so strong!

Every single one of us has fallen overboard, and *every single one of us* is in over our head. Struggling to stay afloat in the freezing water, we face the fact that we are lost at sea and that we can't survive on our own. We need to be rescued. We need someone to save our souls.

The Best or the Dust? Chosen or Frozen?

We thought we were so strong, and now we're lost, overboard, and completely helpless. Teenagers have been told many times at youth conferences, "You're a chosen generation" and "You were saved for the last days." These are inspiring ideas, but contrast them with the statement of Moses after talking with the Lord, "Now, for this cause I know that man is nothing, which thing I never had supposed" (Moses 1:10), and the statement in Helaman 12:7: "O how great is the nothingness of the children of men; yea, even they are less than the dust of the earth."

So which one is it? Chosen generation, or less than the dust? The answer is: both. Sure, we have a divine nature and divine potential, but we also have a fallen nature that needs to be changed. So how do we go from the "nothing-ness" spoken of in ancient scriptures to the "chosen generation" spoken of by modern prophets? Well, one comes before the other. First, we recognize our fallen nature, our weakness, and our total dependence on the Savior. We put aside our selfishness and pride, and we come to Christ. When we do this first, he can work with us, cleanse us, transform us, and make more out of our lives than we could make out of them by ourselves. He can change our fallen nature and help us reach that divine potential of which so many modern prophets have spoken. But we must come to him first.

A Fall Overboard, the Fall of Adam, and the Fall of Me

We've been taught the doctrine all our lives, but for many of us it really doesn't sink in until we realize we're sunk! The doctrine is called the Fall, and although we're not responsible for it, we're all affected by it. Because of the Fall of Adam, each of us experiences what has been called the "fall of me." From Adam we have inherited a fallen nature, and eventually we all sin and come short of the glory of God (see Romans 3:23). We simply cannot get home in safety by ourselves.

All of us must come to the conclusion that we are totally, completely, and utterly helpless and at the mercy of the only one who can rescue us. In desperation, we send the distress call,

"SOS"—in other words, "we need help, please save our souls."

Jesus can save us. He is the *only* one, or, as the scriptures say, "the only name . . . given under heaven" that can save (Moses 6:52). In fact, that is why he has a very special life-saving title: *Savior.* Because he saves! Although many of us are baptized at age eight, receive the gift of the Holy Ghost, and attend church faithfully, it is more often later in life when we come to understand Jesus as our *Savior* and not just "our best friend" or someone cheering for us in heaven.

Brother Robert L. Millet has written: "Jesus is far more than a celestial cheerleader; he is my only hope for peace here and eternal life hereafter. Jesus is far more than a spiritual adviser; he is the sinless Son of Man who bids me to become as he is. Jesus is far more than a model of sane living; his is the power by which I may be reclaimed, regenerated, and renewed, changed into a new creature, a new creature alive in Christ" (*Alive in Christ* [Deseret Book, 1997], 13).

Say to them that are of a fearful heart, Be strong, fear not: behold, your God will come. . . . He will come and save you.

—Isaiah 35:4

The Good Shepherd thus comes on a search-and-rescue mission after all of his lost sheep. He who never took a moral detour or a backward step thus reaches out and reaches down to lift us up. We are lost in the sense that we have wandered from a more exalted sphere; in the sense that we do not know our way home without a guide.

—Robert L. Millet, in *Nurturing Faith through the Book of Mormon* (Deseret Book, 1995), 123

By Grace or By Works?

Critics of the Church often say that Mormons believe they can "earn their way to heaven." They're wrong. We're drowning in the sea, and there's no way we can swim all the way home or "earn" our way to eternal life.

President David O. McKay taught: "In this old world of ours, children of men are . . . struggling in the sea of life. There are those who claim that no one will sink and be lost if he will look to Jesus on the shore and say, 'I believe.' [Saved by grace alone.] There are others who declare that everyone must by his own efforts swim to the shore or be lost forever. [Saved by works alone.] The real truth is that both of these extreme views are incorrect. Christ will not save men who will put forth no effort themselves. . . . Neither can man save himself without accepting the means provided by Christ for man's salvation" (*Gospel Ideals* [Improvement Era, 1953], 549).

The opportunity to repent is like a buoyant life preserver thrown to us and landing within our reach. What a welcome sight! We don't "earn" the life preserver. It appears as an act of pure mercy. It is provided for us because of the Atonement of Jesus Christ. He knew of our fall and has been on a search-and-rescue mission to save our souls.

What must we do? Well, that's pretty obvious, isn't it? We hold on! We exercise faith that he can save us, and then we do what he asks! We repent of our sins, submit to baptism, receive the gift of the Holy Ghost, and endure to the end by keeping our covenants. These essential parts of the saving gospel are included within what is often called the "doctrine of Christ" (see 2 Nephi 31).

Have I Been Saved?

Some of us have a hard time remembering exactly *when* we were saved. Perhaps we were so busy trying to stay afloat that we didn't realize what was happening! Actually, that's the way it is for most people. To be sure, there are some whose rescue from the Fall is quite dramatic—Alma the Younger, Paul, and Enos, for example. But the rest of us may experience something a little less remarkable.

President Ezra Taft Benson taught: "The scriptures record remarkable accounts of men whose lives changed dramatically, in an instant, as it were: Alma the Younger, Paul on the road to Damascus, Enos praying far into the night, King Lamoni. . . . But we must be cautious as we discuss these remarkable examples. Though they are real and powerful, they are the exception more than the rule. For every Paul, for every Enos, and for every King Lamoni, there are hundreds and thousands of people who find the process of repentance much more subtle, much more imperceptible. Day by day they move closer to the Lord, little realizing they are building a godlike life. They live quiet lives of goodness, service, and commitment. They are like the Lamanites, who the Lord said 'were baptized with fire and with the Holy Ghost, *and they knew it not.*' (3 Ne. 9:20; italics added)" (in *Repentance* [Deseret Book, 1990], 6–7)

Some teens feel like they're not making any spiritual headway, and they're waiting for some dramatic event to cause a "mighty change." They may not recognize the progress they've already made. Things they used to say, like, "I can't see that movie," or "I can't wear that dress," have slowly changed to "I don't *want* to see that movie," and "I don't *want* to dress like that." They're not perfect, but little by little, their hearts are changing, and they're losing their desire to sin. The power of the rescuing atonement is already active in their lives; they just haven't recognized it!

The Captain's on the Bridge!

Removed from the icy water and warmed by the love of our Savior, we are soon restored to our ship. He came that we might have life, and that we might have it more abundantly. He atoned for our sins so that we could be "at one" with him and the Father. We're so glad he came! We stand all amazed at his love for us. We feel so overwhelmed by his mercy that we just want to follow him. Our hearts have been changed. We have no more disposition to do evil (see Mosiah 5:2). We have been reborn! He has saved our souls.

Something else has changed: We sense that we are no longer in command. We have been saved by the Savior, and now we must be led by the Lord. *Lord* is another of Jesus' special titles. We can't call him *Lord* and then not do the things that he says. Calling him *Lord* means we want *him* to be in command of our lives. We want what *he* wants. *He* is the captain of our souls.

We also feel we should change the name on our ship. When we were born, our parents gave us a name. But when we're born again, we take upon us the name of Christ. We've made a covenant to stand as witnesses of God at all times, in all things, and in all places. Truly, our Captain has made a lot of changes.

President Ezra Taft Benson taught: "Yes, Christ changes men, and changed men can change the world. Men changed for Christ will be captained by Christ. Like Paul they will be asking, 'Lord, what wilt thou have me to do?' (Acts 9:6). Peter stated they will 'follow his steps' (1 Peter 2:21). John said they will 'walk, even as he walked' (1 John 2:6). Finally, men captained by Christ will be consumed in Christ" (*A Witness and a Warning*, 64).

God is at the helm. He guides the ship, and will bring us safely into port. All we have to care about is to take care of ourselves and see that we do right.

Let us man the ship manfully, everyone standing faithfully and firmly to his post, and she will outride every storm and safely bear us to the harbor of celestial bliss.

—Brigham Young,
The Man and His Work
(Deseret Book, 1936), 352

Steady—
or Steadfast—
As She Goes

The Savior has calmed the storms and filled our hearts with faith and hope, and now we can prepare to resume our journey back home.

We have been taught about the Savior all our lives, but because of our recent rescue, he is much more real to us now. We recognize our dependence on him. And although he is not physically present, we know he is near, to "lead us, guide us, and walk beside us." We will "press forward with a steadfastness in Christ, having a perfect brightness of hope, and a love of God and of all men" (2 Nephi 31:20).

No doubt there will be more storms and dangers ahead, but keeping our covenants will keep us on course. The Prophet Joseph Smith taught:

"You know, brethren, that a very large ship is benefited very much by a very small helm in the time of a storm, by being kept workways with the wind and the waves. Therefore, . . . let us cheerfully do all things that lie in our power; and then may we stand still, with the utmost assurance, to see the salvation of God, and for his arm to be revealed" (D&C 123:16–17).

So that's what we'll do. That "very small helm" is what enables us to stay on course. We'll do the best we can and rely on the Lord to see us through. Elder M. Russell Ballard taught: "Let us remember that the Savior is the Way, the Truth, and the Life, and there can be no greater promise than to know that if we are faithful and true, we will one day be safely encircled in the arms of His love (see D&C 6:20). He is always there to give us encouragement, to forgive, and to rescue. Therefore, as we exercise faith and are diligent in keeping the commandments, we have nothing to fear in the journey" (*Ensign,* May 1997, 61).

Light the Way!

We've been rescued! Jesus has saved our souls. Once again, we stand on the deck with the wind at our backs. Our clothes are fresh and dry, and our hearts are filled with a new sense of peace and assurance. Now we can happily resume our journey back home.

Not only do we enjoy the constant direction of our compass but we can also rely on another constant—the steady beam from an immovable lighthouse, the shining example of Jesus Christ. He said, "Therefore, hold up your light that it may shine unto the world. Behold I am the light which ye shall hold up—that which ye have seen me do" (3 Nephi 18:24).

There are other lights *in* the world, but none can compare with the Light *of* the World. In the words of the hymn "Beautiful Savior":

Fair is the sunshine,
Fairer the moonlight,

and all the stars in heav'n above;
Jesus shines brighter,
Jesus shines purer
And brings to all the world His love.
(*Children's Songbook* [The Church of Jesus Christ of
     Latter-day Saints, 1989], 62–63)

In 1833 an Englishman named John Henry
Newman became deathly ill on the island of
Sicily. He longed to return home to England,
where he thought he might become well. On the
first leg of his voyage, the winds ceased, the fog
closed in, and his ship made no progress for a
week. Homesick, seasick, and afflicted with
malaria, he wrote these words:

Lead, kindly Light, amid th'encircling gloom;
Lead thou me on!
The night is dark, and I am far from home;
Lead thou me on!
(*Hymns*, no. 97; see Karen Lynn Davidson, *Our
Latter-Day Hymns* [Deseret Book, 1988], 126).

Indeed, the warming, kindly light of the
Savior is the lighthouse that will lead us home
through darkness and gloom.

What's the Current Thing?

Without our maps, our compass, and a sense of direction, we drift with the currents. We go where they take us. And it may not be where we want to go. Some teens don't care. They don't think about what's best, they just think about what's current. They go with the flow.

What is current at your school? Some are swept along in the current pursuit of popularity. How they are perceived and treated by others is most important. They want to be seen with the right people. They say "hi" only to those in the current group.

Others are caught in the current quest for "stuff." We are hip-deep in Roller-blades, Play-stations, Walkmans, and CDs. But we always seem to want more. When we have enough, we want more than enough. The current of materialism is strong and it never stops pulling.

The problem with being at the mercy of the currents is that the currents are not merciful. You may wind up far from home. It may be that the currents are cheating people's souls and leading them carefully away from home. It doesn't seem like it, though. Drifting along with a questionable current is often defended with these words: "Everybody does it," or "Who cares?"

Mormon describes those who cease to be led by God and are led by other currents in these words: "But now, behold, they are led about by Satan . . . as a vessel is tossed about upon the waves, without sail or anchor, or without anything wherewith to steer her; and even as she is, so are they" (Mormon 5:18).

Our power to move in the direction we choose must be able to overcome the power of the currents.

The time is coming and facing you right now, you young people, when except you have that testimony of certainty that these things [the gospel, the Church, and so on] are true you will not be able to weather the storms that are going to beat upon you and try to tear you from your moorings today.

But if you know with all your soul that these things are true that we have been talking about, you will know who Jesus your Savior is and who God your Father is; you will know what the influence of the Holy Ghost is. If you know those things you will stand as an anchor against all the storms that shall beat upon [you].

—*Teachings of Harold B. Lee*
(Bookcraft, 1996), 140

An Anchor to Weather the Storms

Sometimes, when the weather ahead looks rough, we need to search for a quiet cove or natural harbor where we can let down our anchors and ride out the storm.

Every one of us needs something to keep us anchored to what is lasting and true. Several years ago, my brother and his wife endured a severe storm. As long as I live, I will never forget the experience of watching my brother carry in his arms a tiny white coffin. It was his son, a baby boy that he and his wife had been so excited to welcome into their home. The baby died inside his mother, two days before he was due to be born.

As I watched my brother, I wondered, "What's helping him through it?" Was he thinking to himself, "Well, at least I was popular in high school"? Of course not. Was he thinking, "Well, at least I have nice clothes"? No. Was he thinking, "Good thing I have a lot of material things"? He wasn't. Suddenly all the "current" things, the things that people worry so much about, meant nothing. Absolutely nothing.

What was his anchor? My brother and his wife have a *testimony*. They know the plan of salvation! They believe in Jesus Christ, who died so that all might live again, including their little boy.

Even with a true anchor, the storm was painful, and the aftermath was very difficult. But there is nothing, absolutely nothing, like the anchor of the gospel of Jesus Christ. The anchor of testimony is *power,* real power for enduring the most difficult storms this life can produce. With that anchor, the mighty storms that beat upon you will have "no power over you to drag you down to the gulf of misery and endless wo" (Helaman 5:12).

Remaining Seaworthy

The Savior has cleansed our sins and saved our souls. We remain worthy and on course by keeping our covenants.

A covenant is a two-way promise. When we keep our covenants, not only are we protected from the consequences of sin but the Lord promises to help us overcome by sending his Spirit to guide us.

Keeping our covenants helps us remain seaworthy. Our covenants are a watertight protection, and we don't want any leaks!

All the water in the world,
However hard it tried,
Could never sink the smallest ship
Unless it got inside.
And all the evil in the world,
The blackest kind of sin,
Can never hurt you the least bit
Unless you let it in.

(Author unknown, in *Best Loved Poems of The LDS People,* ed. Jack M. Lyon et al. [Deseret Book, 1996], 302)

Sailors sometimes use an instrument called a sextant to help them find their position on the earth. It measures the constant position of the stars against the horizon and tells the navigators where they are.

President Boyd K. Packer taught: "The mariner gets his bearings from light coming from celestial bodies—the sun by day, the stars by night. . . . The spiritual sextant, which each of us has, also functions on the principle of light from celestial sources. Set that sextant in your mind to the word *covenant* or the word *ordinance.* The light will come through. Then you can fix your position and set a true course in life" (*Ensign,* April 1987, 26–27).

Keeping covenants keeps us on course.

Sail On!

Now that we have made covenants and are striving to keep them, our main focus is to endure to the end (see Mark 13:13).

Do we have to be perfect to make it home in safety? Nope. We're not perfect, and at times we may get a little off course. So we repent, renew our covenants, and get back on course. We've already been saved, and all that remains is that we sail on and endure to the end.

Elder Dallin H. Oaks taught: "I have suggested that the short answer to the question of whether a faithful member of The Church of Jesus Christ of Latter-day Saints has been saved or born again must be a fervent, 'yes.' Our covenant relationship with our Savior puts us in that 'saved' or 'born again' condition meant by those who ask this question" (*Ensign,* May 1998, 57).

What do we do now? We *strive,* we *stay the course,* we *sail on!* We do what Columbus did. President Ezra Taft Benson spoke of his perseverance in these words: "Four hundred and sixty-seven years ago Christopher Columbus set sail from Spain in three small ships with eighty-seven men. For seventy days they sailed across the uncharted sea. As early as the seventeenth day the men began to murmur in fear. From the twentieth day on, Columbus was hard put to restrain them from mutiny, but when we read the log that Columbus kept, we are struck by the force of three words appearing again and again at the end of the day's events; these are the words, 'We sailed on.' What courage, what trustworthiness, what faith these words reveal!" (*So Shall Ye Reap* [Deseret Book, 1960], 141).

That's exactly what we need as well: courage to keep our covenants, trust and faith in the Lord and his saving power. We sail on!

Family Reunion

Some voyages are short, and some are long. Some of us return home sooner than expected. But all of us are on our way to the same destination.

There are many, many days ahead on our way home. There are numerous trials and storms in our future as well. But we know what to do! We have our map, our compass, our anchor, and our lighthouse. Most important, the Savior is the Captain of our souls! We sail on!

Someday we'll be home again. We'll reach the safe harbor of our Heavenly Father's home. That wonderful moment is expressed in the last verse of the hymn "O My Father":

Then, at length, when I've completed
All you sent me forth to do,
With your mutual approbation
Let me come and dwell with you.
             (*Hymns*, no. 292)

What a reunion that will be! Can you imagine all the people you will meet? Do you think anything will surprise you? What do you think will startle you the most? President Ezra Taft Benson taught, "Nothing is going to startle us more, when we pass through the veil to the other side, than to realize how well we know our Father, and how familiar his face is to us" (*Teachings of Ezra Taft Benson*, 24).

Familiar. That's the perfect word to use because it comes from the same root as the word *family.* His face will be familiar. He's our Father. We're his children. We're a family! And we've come home.